Baby Blues® **10** Scrapbook

threats, &bribes, & videotape

W9-AWH-510

Other Baby Blues® books from Andrews McMeel Publishing

Guess Who Didn't Take a Nap?
I Thought Labor Ended When the Baby Was Born
We Are Experiencing Parental Difficulties. . . Please Stand By
Night of the Living Dad
I Saw Elvis in My Ultrasound
One More and We're Outnumbered!
Check, Please. . .

Treasury

The Super-Absorbent Biodegradable Family-Size Baby Blues®

Baby Blues® **10** Scrapbook

threats, & bribes & videotape

by Rick Kirkman & Jerry Scott

Andrews McMeel
Publishing
Kansas City

Baby Blues is syndicated internationally by King Features Syndicate, Inc. For information, write King Features Syndicate, Inc., 216 East 45th Street, New York, New York 10017.

threats, bribes & videotape copyright © 1998 by Baby Blues Partnership. All rights reserved. Printed in the United States of America. No part of this book may be used or reproduced in any manner whatsoever without written permission except in the case of reprints in the context of reviews. For information, write Andrews McMeel Publishing, an Andrews McMeel Universal company, 4520 Main Street, Kansas City, Missouri 64111.

www.andrewsmcmeel.com

99 00 01 02 BAH 10 9 8 7 6 5 4 3

ISBN: 0-8362-6750-8

Library of Congress Catalog Card Number: 98-85358

——————— **ATTENTION: SCHOOLS AND BUSINESSES** ———————

Andrews McMeel books are available at quantity discounts with bulk purchase for educational, business, or sales promotional use. For information, please write to: Special Sales Department, Andrews McMeel Publishing, 4520 Main Street, Kansas City, Missouri 64111.

To Kim and Abbey, the loves of my life.

—J.S.

Once again, for Sukey, who deserves more recognition than this.

To my Mom and Dad, tireless promoters of my work.

And thanks to the members of the National Cartoonists Society for
the last decade of inspiration, encouragement, and hospitality.

—R.K.

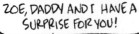

Panel 1: ZOE, DADDY AND I HAVE A SURPRISE FOR YOU!

Panel 2: GRANDMA AND GRANDPA ARE COMING HERE FOR THANKSGIVING, AND WE'RE GOING TO LET THEM SLEEP IN YOUR ROOM!

Panel 3: AND THAT MEANS YOU GET TO SLEEP ON THE FLOOR IN HAMMIE'S ROOM! WON'T THAT BE GREAT??

Panel 4: HOW WAS THAT? / A LITTLE TOO ENTHUSIASTIC... TRY SMILING WITHOUT SHOWING YOUR MOLARS.

Panel 5: ZOE! GRANDMA AND GRANDPA ARE HERE! / YAY!!!

Panel 6: GWANDMA! GWANDPA! / THERE'S MY GIRL! / HI, SWEETHEART!

Panel 7: POP! I TOLD YOU NOT TO BRING HER ANY CANDY!

Panel 8: I KNOW, BUT I THOUGHT ONE PIECE WOULD BE OKAY... / I WIFE HIM!

Panel 9: MO' CANDY, GWANDPA? / HEE-HEE! SURE! / POP, THAT'S THE FIFTH PIECE OF CANDY SHE'S HAD THIS MORNING!

Panel 10: WELL, KIDS WILL BE KIDS... / YEAH, BUT I WOULDN'T WANT HER TO OVERDO IT, AND...UH... I DID ASK YOU TO TAKE IT EASY...SO...

Panel 11: WHACK! / PUT THE CANDY AWAY, MAC!

Panel 12: OKIE-DOKIE. / THE OLDER THEY GET, THE LESS TACTFUL YOU HAVE TO BE. / I'LL REMEMBER THAT.

MOM?...POP? WHY DON'T WE ALL JOIN HANDS FOR THE BLESSING?

OOF! ERK! AGH! UNHH!

ON SECOND THOUGHT, MAYBE WE DIDN'T NEED TO PUT ALL THREE LEAVES IN THE TABLE...

HURRY UP AND PRAY, SON! MY SHOULDERS ARE GOING NUMB!

KIRKMAN & SCOTT

I WONDER IF WANDA NEEDS ANY HELP WITH THE DISHES?

I DOUBT IT...YOUR MOTHER IS IN THERE.

I WONDER IF SHE NEEDS ANY HELP WITH THE KIDS?

I DOUBT IT...YOUR MOTHER IS IN THERE.

KIRKMAN & SCOTT

I WONDER IF SHE NEEDS ANY HELP WITH MOM?

NOW **THAT'S** A POSSIBILITY...

ARE YOU SURE YOU HAVE TO LEAVE ALREADY?

YES...WE PROMISED AUNT MIN A VISIT, AND IT'S A TWO-HOUR DRIVE.

SHE BROKE HER HIP, YOU KNOW, AND HASN'T BEEN GETTING AROUND VERY WELL. NOW, IF SHE LISTENED TO HER DOCTOR SHE WOULD BE MUCH BETTER OFF, BUT YOU KNOW AUNT MIN. OF COURSE, THE DOCTORS ALL LOOK LIKE KIDS TODAY, SO WHO CAN BLAME HER? I REMEMBER WHEN I HAD MY HYSTERECTOMY...

COME ON, MOTHER! IT'S LATE!

DADDY'S RIGHT. WE'D BETTER GET GOING IF WE PLAN ON GETTING OUT OF THERE BEFORE DARK.

YOU KNOW HOW AUNT MIN IS... TALK, TALK, TALK...

KIRKMAN & SCOTT

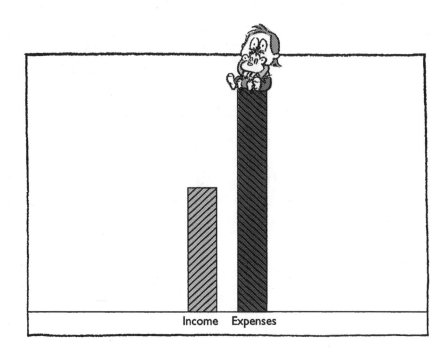

11

=SIGH!=

WANDA? HONEY? ARE YOU OKAY? WHAT'S WRONG?

IS THERE SOMETHING I CAN DO TO HELP? NAME IT! I'LL DO ANYTHING!

STAY HOME AND TAKE CARE OF THE KIDS WHILE I GO TO WORK, EAT LUNCH IN RESTAURANTS, TALK TO ADULTS, AND WEAR NICE CLOTHES FOR A CHANGE.

OKAY... ALMOST ANYTHING.

THANKS FOR GIVING ME SOME TIME TO MYSELF, DARRYL. I FEEL MUCH BETTER.

I'M SORRY I WAS SUCH A BLUBBERING BASKET CASE EARLIER. THE KIDS JUST HAD ME AT THE END OF MY ROPE.

IT'S KIND OF SILLY, NOW THAT I THINK ABOUT IT. IMAGINE! A COUPLE OF SWEET LITTLE KIDS MAKING A GROWN PERSON CRY!

=SNIFF!=

DO YOU HAVE TO GO POTTY, ZOE?

YES.

DO YOU NEED ANY HE—

NO! I DON'T NEED HELP! I'M A BIG GIRL! YOU WAIT HERE!

=SLAM!=

CAN YOU LIFT ME UP?

12

BABY BLUES

by RICK KIRKMAN / JERRY SCOTT

13

16

HI, WIDDLE BABY! ARE YOU HUNGWY?

MOMMY HAS YOUR CEWEAL... HEY! DON'T CHEW THAT!

NYUNG NYUNG

STOP GWABBING MY STUFF! GIMME DAT! STOP! YOU'RE DWIVING ME CWAZY!!

PRETTY CUTE, DON'T YOU THINK?

I WAS GOING TO USE THE WORD "FAMILIAR."

GRRRR

DID YOU HEAR SOMETHING?

LIKE WHAT?

THERE WAS A SOFT "THUMP," THEN A BUNCH OF TINY "PIT-PATS," FOLLOWED BY A "CLANK" THAT SOUNDED LIKE THE COOKIE JAR LID, MORE "PIT-PATS," AND A SOFT "CRUNCH" SOUND.

YOU DIDN'T HEAR THAT...

NO.

I THINK YOU'RE IMAGINING THINGS.

ME TOO. TURN IT UP.

EAT YOUR PEAS.

I DON'T WIKE PEAS.

SURE YOU DO! YOU'VE ALWAYS LIKED PEAS! PEAS ARE YOUR FAVORITE VEGETABLE, REMEMBER?

OH YEAH... I FORGOT. I DO WIKE PEAS!

I JUST DON'T WIKE THESE PEAS.

YOUR TURN.

Panel 1: IS THERE ANYTHING I CAN DO TO HELP YOU, HONEY? / NO, DEAR. YOU'VE HAD A HARD DAY...

Panel 2: WHY DON'T YOU JUST GO IN THE LIVING ROOM AND PUT YOUR FEET UP WHILE I FINISH THE DISHES, GET THE KIDS READY FOR BED, CLEAN UP THE LIVING ROOM, DO A COUPLE OF LOADS OF LAUNDRY, AND WASH THE CAR.

Panel 3: WELL... OKAY! THANKS!

Panel 4: YOU'D THINK AFTER THIS MANY YEARS OF MARRIAGE, I'D BE ABLE TO RECOGNIZE SARCASM.

KIRKMAN & SCOTT

Panel 5: THIS IS DISGUSTING! / I WANT DAT! AND DAT! AND DAT! AND DAT, TOO!

Panel 6: THESE COMMERCIALS THEY RUN RIGHT BEFORE CHRISTMAS ARE CRIMINAL!

Panel 7: THEY'RE LOUDER, FLASHIER, AND OBVIOUSLY MEANT TO CAPTURE THE ATTENTION OF THE WEAKER, MORE IMPRESSIONABLE MINDS AMONG US!

Panel 8: I'M TURNING IT OFF... / WAIT... I WANT TO SEE THIS... OOH, THAT'S **NICE**...

KIRKMAN & SCOTT

Panel 9: REMEMBER A COUPLE OF YEARS AGO WHEN OUR CHRISTMAS CARDS WENT OUT LATE, SO WE WROTE "HAPPY HOLIDAYS" INSTEAD OF "MERRY CHRISTMAS" INSIDE? / YEP.

Panel 10: AND THEN THE NEXT YEAR WE WERE EVEN LATER, SO "HAPPY HOLIDAYS" BECAME "SEASON'S GREETINGS"? / HA! YEAH.

Panel 11:

KIRKMAN & SCOTT

Panel 12: ANY IDEAS FOR THIS YEAR? / HOW ABOUT "HAPPY EASTER"?

IT'S DECEMBER 24th, ZOE!

REALLY?!

TONIGHT IS THE NIGHT THAT EIGHT REINDEER AND RUDOLPH WILL LAND ON OUR ROOF, AND SANTA CLAUS WILL SLIDE DOWN OUR CHIMNEY WITH A BIG BAG OF TOYS FOR YOU!

WOW!!

TOMORROW MORNING THERE WILL BE LOTS OF PRESENTS AND CANDY UNDER THE CHRISTMAS TREE FOR YOU AND HAMMIE TO OPEN!

YAY!!!

OH BOY! TOYS! OH BOY! TOYS! OH BOY! TOYS!

THE MEDIA SHOULD BE ASHAMED FOR TURNING THIS INTO SUCH A COMMERCIAL HOLIDAY.

CHRISTMAS — 6:00AM

CHRISTMAS — 7:00AM

CHRISTMAS — 7:01AM

IS DAT ALL?

AUNT WONDA! AUNT WONDA!

HI, KIDDO!

MEWWY KWISMUS!

WOW! WELL, MERRY CHRISTMAS TO YOU, TOO, SWEETIE!

÷ SNIFF! ÷ LEAVE IT TO A CHILD TO REMIND US WHAT CHRISTMAS IS REALLY ABOUT!

YOU CAN SAY THAT AGAIN.

WHADJA GET ME?

21

I WISH YOU'D ASKED US BEFORE YOU BOUGHT ZOE A BARBIE DOLL FOR CHRISTMAS, RHONDA.

WHY? WHAT'S WRONG WITH IT?

ZOE'S ONLY TWO-AND-A-HALF YEARS OLD! SHE NEEDS TIME TO BE A KID BEFORE SHE STARTS PLAYING WITH SOME HIGHLY SEXUALIZED, FASHION-DRIVEN SYMBOL OF MATERIALISTIC EXCESS LIKE BARBIE!

OH COME ON! DO YOU HONESTLY THINK A SMART LITTLE KID LIKE ZOE CAN BE AFFECTED BY A SILLY PLASTIC DOLL?

LOOK! BOOBIES!

MAYBE...

KIRKMAN & SCOTT

¿SIGH!¿

¿SIGH!¿

DO YOU FEEL OKAY?

I THINK I HAVE POST-HOLIDAY CATALOG WITHDRAWAL.

KIRKMAN & SCOTT

DO YOU THINK IT WAS RIGHT TO TELL ZOE THAT HER BARBIE DOLL IS A HORRIBLE FREAK OF NATURE?

AAARGGH! EEK! HELP! HELP!

WHY NOT?

BARBIE REPRESENTS A WARPED VIEW OF WOMEN! IN ORDER FOR A WOMAN TO HAVE BARBIE'S BODY, SHE WOULD HAVE TO BE OVER SEVEN FEET TALL, WEIGH 120 POUNDS, HAVE A 15-INCH WAIST AND A 47-INCH BUST!!

CAN YOU IMAGINE??

GIVE ME A MINUTE...

KIRKMAN & SCOTT

22

BABY BLUES®

BY RICK KIRKMAN / JERRY SCOTT

WHAT DO YOU THINK?

I DON'T KNOW... IT'S UP TO YOU.

WELL, IF WE WAIT UNTIL NEW YEAR'S TO TAKE THE CHRISTMAS TREE DOWN, THE NEEDLES ARE GOING TO START FALLING OFF AND MAKE A HUGE MESS IN HERE.

OKAY.

REMEMBER LAST YEAR? I WAS STILL VACUUMING UP PINE NEEDLES AT EASTER!

UH-HUH.

PLUS, WE WON'T FEEL LIKE DOING IT ON THE FIRST BECAUSE WE'RE GOING OUT WITH RHONDA ON NEW YEAR'S EVE.

GOOD POINT.

BESIDES, THESE THINGS BECOME A REAL FIRE HAZARD WHEN THEY DRY OUT!

YEP.

I SAW A REPORT ON THE NEWS WHERE THEY PUT A MATCH TO A DRY TREE LIKE THIS, AND IT BURNED IN THREE SECONDS!

I KNOW.

KIRKMAN & SCOTT

WHAT A RELIEF TO HAVE THAT OUT OF THE WAY! NOW WE DON'T HAVE TO WORRY ABOUT IT ANY MORE.

HEY! WHERE'S DA KWISMUS TWEE?!

I HOPE YOU'RE HAPPY.

SO, WHERE ARE YOU GUYS GOING FOR NEW YEAR'S EVE?

WE'RE THERE.

YOU MEAN YOU'RE STAYING HOME AGAIN?? **DARRYL!**

WHAT?? WE **LIKE** STAYING HOME!

WE DON'T HAVE TO GET DRESSED UP... WE DON'T HAVE TO DRIVE ANYWHERE... WE DON'T HAVE TO SPEND ANY MONEY...

...WE DON'T HAVE TO DANCE... WE DON'T HAVE TO EAT A NICE MEAL... WE DON'T HAVE TO HAVE FUN...

SEE? WANDA AGREES WITH ME!

DO YOU THINK I SHOULD WEAR THIS LONG DRESS OR THE LITTLE BLACK ONE?

THEY'RE BOTH KIND OF DRESSY, AREN'T THEY?

NOT FOR A NEW YEAR'S EVE PARTY... RHONDA SAID IT'S BLACK TIE, REMEMBER?

DO I REALLY **HAVE** TO WEAR THE TUX?

YES, YOU **HAVE** TO WEAR THE TUX... **AND** THE TIE... **AND** GOOD SHOES... **AND** THE CUMMERBUND. ANY OTHER QUESTIONS?

DO WE HAVE TO STAY OUT LATE?

MY FIRST CHANCE IN AGES TO GREET **BABY NEW YEAR**, AND MY DATE IS **FATHER TIME.**

WE'RE LEAVING NOW. I WANT YOU TO PROMISE ME THAT YOU'LL BE GOOD TONIGHT.

THAT MEANS NO WHINING, NO POUTING, NO COMPLAINING, AND NO TANTRUMS... GOT THAT?

AND THAT GOES FOR YOU GUYS, TOO.

24

25

Baby Blues

BY RICK KIRKMAN / JERRY SCOTT

1. DEAR AUNT RHONDA...

YEAH... DAT'S GOOD.

2. THANK YOU FOR THE GREAT CHRISTMAS PRESENT.

UH-HUH.

3. IT IS MY VERY FIRST BARBIE® DOLL, AND I PLAY WITH IT EVERY DAY. LOVE, ZOE

4. DOES THAT SOUND OKAY?

YEP! BYE!

DID YOU MENTION YOU TOLD ZOE THAT BARBIE® IS A FREAK OF NATURE, NOT THE STANDARD OF BEAUTY?

IS THAT REALLY RELEVANT?

AIEEEEEE

IT'S BARBIE®!! RUN, TEDDY! RUN!!

KIRKMAN & SCOTT

OKAY, KIDS... LET'S ALL SING!

♪ HAPPY BIRTHDAY TO YOU... ♪

JINGLE BELLS! JINGLE BELLS!

♪ THE WHEELS ON THE BUS GO 'ROUND AND 'ROUND! ♪

♪ LONDON BRIDGE IS FAWWING DOWN... ♪

ITSY-BITSY SPIDER...

ACTUALLY, I MEANT THAT WE SHOULD ALL SING THE SAME SONG...

NOW CAN WE BLOW UP THE CANDLES?

EASY, BUD...

WELL, OUR LITTLE GIRL IS THREE YEARS OLD.

YEP, HARD TO BELIEVE, ISN'T IT?

IT SEEMS LIKE JUST YESTERDAY THAT SHE WAS A TINY BABY... HELPLESS AND UNAWARE OF THE WORLD AROUND HER.

THINGS SURE CHANGE, DON'T THEY?

ZOE, WILL YOU BRING ME THAT PLATE AND CUP OVER THERE?

OF COURSE, THE MORE THEY CHANGE, THE MORE THEY STAY THE SAME...

ZOE?... ZOE?... HELLO-O-O-O-O!

OPEN UP! OPEN! OPEN!

ZOE, HOW CAN I BRUSH YOUR TEETH IF YOU WON'T OPEN YOUR MOUTH? COME ON! OPEN UP!

¡SNICKER!

I'M SORRY... YOU SHOULD HEAR... IT JUST SOUNDED...

GREAT. IF YOU THINK IT'S SO FUNNY, YOU TRY.

28

BABY BLUES®

BY RICK KIRKMAN / JERRY SCOTT

...AN' I WANNA SLIDE DOWN DA HILL, AN' MAKE A SNOWMAN, AN' FROW SNOWBALLS, AN' DO SNOW ANGELS, AN'...

OKAY! OKAY! JUST LET ME FINISH DRESSING HAMMIE!

FINALLY!

YAY!

KIRKMAN & SCOTT

CLICK!

I'M DONE!

HERE, HAMMIE... WANT A BITE?

NO, ZOE!

HAMMIE ISN'T QUITE READY FOR SOLID FOOD, SWEETHEART.

BESIDES, LITTLE BABIES ONLY EAT FOOD THAT HAS BEEN MASHED.

OH....

KIRKMAN & SCOTT

HERE, ZOE... LET DADDY HELP YOU WITH THAT MILK.

I CAN DO IT MYSELF!

BUT IT'S REALLY FULL, AND I—

IT'S MINE!

OKAY! IT'S YOURS! JUST LET ME GIVE YOU A H—

STOP!

NOW LOOK WHAT YOU DID!

KIRKMAN & SCOTT

I INVITED THE BREWERS OVER FOR DINNER ON WEDNESDAY.

THE **BREWERS**? THE PEOPLE WITH THAT PROBLEM WHERE THEY CAN'T HAVE KIDS?

THE TERM IS INFERTILITY. AND, YES, THAT'S THEM.

BUT CAN'T YOU FIND A BETTER WAY TO REFER TO THEM THAN IN TERMS OF WHETHER OR NOT THEY HAVE CHILDREN?

YEAH... SURE... LET'S SEE...

HOW ABOUT, "THE COUPLE THAT GETS A FULL NIGHT'S SLEEP?" OR, "THE COUPLE WITH DISPOSABLE INCOME?" OR, "THE COUPLE WITH DECENT FURNITURE?"...

I THINK IT'S GREAT THAT WE'RE HAVING THE BREWERS OVER FOR DINNER, BUT WHAT ARE WE GOING TO TALK ABOUT?

WHAT DO YOU MEAN?

EVER SINCE YOU TOLD ME THAT THEY ARE HAVING FERTILITY PROBLEMS, I DON'T KNOW WHAT TO SAY TO THEM.

OH, COME ON!

YOU SAY THE SAME THINGS YOU WOULD TO PEOPLE WHO HAVE KIDS...

...EXCEPT YOU CAN SPEAK FASTER AND USE BIGGER WORDS.

HEE HEE HEE HEE!

WHAT? I DIDN'T GET THAT...

LOOK, YOU TWO DON'T HAVE TO AVOID TALKING ABOUT YOUR KIDS JUST BECAUSE **WE** CAN'T HAVE CHILDREN.

THAT'S RIGHT. INFERTILITY ISN'T A DISEASE.

WE MAY NEVER BE ABLE TO HAVE KIDS OF OUR OWN, BUT THAT DOESN'T MEAN WE LOVE CHILDREN ANY LESS.

WOW. THAT'S AN AMAZING ATTITUDE.

YEAH. SO MATURE.

FOR WHAT IT'S WORTH, I THINK YOU TWO WOULD MAKE GREAT PARENTS.

IN FACT, YOU MAY BE OVER-QUALIFIED.

GOOD NIGHT! THANKS FOR COMING OVER!

THE BREWERS ARE REALLY NICE PEOPLE.

ALL THIS TIME I ASSUMED THAT JUST BECAUSE THEY DIDN'T HAVE KIDS THAT THEY WERE SELFISH YUPPIE SCUM—

WHEN, IN FACT, THEY'RE A SWEET COUPLE WITH FERTILITY PROBLEMS.

I SURE LEARNED A LESSON TONIGHT.

DON'T JUDGE A BOOK BY ITS COVER?

SELFISH YUPPIE SCUM IS AN ENDANGERED SPECIES.

CLICK!:

TODAY'S PROGRAM WAS BROUGHT TO YOU BY THE TWELFTH LETTER IN THE ALPHABET AND THE SQUARE ROOT OF SIXTEEN.

PBS

"L" AND "4."

I'M TOO DUMB FOR "SESAME STREET"!

SERIOUSLY, WHEN DO YOU THINK WE SHOULD START WEANING HAMMIE?

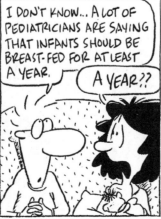

I DON'T KNOW... A LOT OF PEDIATRICIANS ARE SAYING THAT INFANTS SHOULD BE BREAST-FED FOR AT LEAST A YEAR.

A YEAR??

SIX MORE MONTHS?...

WELL, I DON'T THINK PEDIATRICIANS WOULD RECOMMEND IT UNLESS THEY HAD GOOD REASONS.

I DON'T THINK PEDIATRICIANS **SHOULD** RECOMMEND IT UNLESS THEY HAVE **BREASTS!**

SO HOW WAS YOUR DAY?
NOT BAD... BUT THE KIDS WERE ACTING UP IN THE GROCERY STORE.
IT WAS SO WEIRD! ONE MINUTE I HAD A COUPLE OF UNRULY MONSTERS, AND THE NEXT MINUTE I HAD THE SWEETEST, MOST WELL-BEHAVED KIDS IN THE STORE!
KIRKMAN & SCOTT
WOW! HOW DID YOU ACCOMPLISH **THAT**?
I ACCIDENTALLY STARTED PUSHING SOMEONE ELSE'S CART.

DADDY, CAN I HAVE A COOKIE?
I DON'T KNOW... IT'S PRETTY CLOSE TO DINNERTIME. GO ASK MOMMY.
MOMMY?
YES, SWEETIE?
SHE SAID, "YES, SWEETIE."
OH. OKAY.
KIRKMAN & SCOTT

SLAM!
SLAM!
SLAM!
KIRKMAN & SCOTT
WHEN YOU THINK ABOUT IT, WE'VE WASTED A LOT OF MONEY ON DRESSERS AND HANGERS.

IZ YOU MOMMY'S WIDDLE POOKUMS? HMMM?

WELL, YETZ YOU IZ! YETZ YOU IZ! BOOKA-BOOKA-BOOKA!

KIRKMAN & SCOTT

WHEN THEY TAWK LIKE THAT, IT MEANS THEY'RE HAPPY.

WHAT DOES HAMMIE HAVE IN HIS HANDS?

¿SIGH!¿ TRUCKS. HE FOUND THEM IN ZOE'S ROOM THIS MORNING AND HE HASN'T LET GO OF THEM SINCE.

I DON'T THINK HE EVEN PUT THEM DOWN WHILE I FED HIM.

OH... GOOD.

KIRKMAN & SCOTT

THEN THAT EXPLAINS THE TIRE TRACKS ACROSS YOUR CHEST.

TELL DADDY WHAT YOU DID TODAY, ZOE.

WELL FIRSTWEPWAYED CIRCLE AN' WE WENT AROUND - MOMMY WIKES APPLE JUICE TOO! - I SAID, "I HAVE AN IDEA!", AN' SO - KNOW WHAT? BIRDS FWY WA-A-A-Y UP HIGH INNA SKY AN' THEN CUZ WATCHES KNOW WHAT TIME IT IS.

KIRKMAN & SCOTT

DID YOU GET ALL THAT?

I THINK SHE HAS A 200-MEGAHERTZ MIND WITH A 10-MEGAHERTZ MOUTH.

BABY BLUES

RICK KIRKMAN / JERRY SCOTT

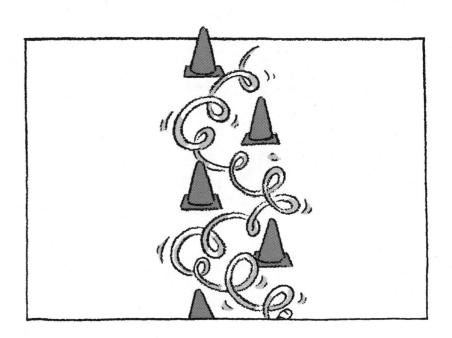

EEEEK! IT'S A MONSTER! QUICK! HIDE!

HANG ON! I'M COMING!!

HYAHH! OOF! SMACK!

PWETEND I'M FAWWING OFFA CWIFF AND YOU DIE SAVING ME.

WE MAY BE WATCHING TOO MANY ANIMATED ADVENTURES AROUND HERE.

I CAN'T BELIEVE THAT HAMMIE ALREADY HAS A TOOTH... DID ZOE GET HER FIRST TOOTH THIS EARLY?

YES. ALMOST EXACTLY THE SAME AGE.

YEAH... I GUESS IT WAS AT SIX MONTHS, BUT IT SEEMED LIKE LONGER.

SIX MONTHS USED TO SEEM LIKE SIX MONTHS... NOW SIX MONTHS SEEMS LIKE SIX WEEKS!

SO IS TIME SPEEDING UP, OR AM I SLOWING DOWN?

DO YOU REALLY WANT TO KNOW?

WHATTER YOU DOING, MOMMY?

PUTTING ON MY MAKEUP.

WHY?

SO I'LL LOOK PRETTY.

BUT YOU'RE ALWEDDY PWETTY!

WANNA HEAR A GOOD WAY TO GET A COOKIE?

ZOE MADE DARRYL THE CUTEST VALENTINE'S CARD...

LET ME SEE.

SHE GLUED ON THE SEQUINS AND PIPE CLEANERS AND PAINTED IT ALL BY HERSELF.

HOW SWEET!

"Roses are red,
Violets are sad.
Take Mommy to dinner.
She needs it real bad."

KIRKMAN & SCOTT

I HELPED WITH THE WORDING.

YOU CAN'T REALLY TELL.

≥AHEM!≤

OOOH! CANDY AND FLOWERS! HOW SWEET!

AND THAT'S NOT ALL...

TA-DAAAH!

≥GASP!≤ OH, DARRYL! JUST WHAT I WANTED...

...A REAL BABY-SITTER!

IT'S JUST A RENTAL... GO GET DRESSED.

HAPPY VALENTINE'S DAY, MRS. MacPHERSON.

I'M REALLY GETTING SICK OF COMMUTING.

I WONDER WHAT IT WOULD BE LIKE TO HAVE A JOB WHERE I COULD BE MY OWN BOSS AND JUST WORK AT HOME...?

OH.

KIRKMAN & SCOTT

VVVV VVVV VVVV VVVV VV-SKNXXTTT!

VVVVV VVVVVV VV-KKX XXVREE EEEEP!

VVVVVVVV VV-XXXXK KPPPHII P-P-P-P-P!!

EVIL PEOPLE SHOULD BE REINCARNATED AS VACUUM CLEANERS IN HOMES WITH CHILDREN.

THWACK!

TRIP! Thunk! SCRAPE!

BONK!

I THINK WE'D BETTER POSTPONE ZOE'S CHECKUP.

YEAH... SHE LOOKS TOO MUCH LIKE SHE NEEDS TO SEE A DOCTOR TO GO SEE THE DOCTOR.

YES, SWEETHEART?

DADDY?

DO YOU... UM... DO YOU... UMMM... DO YOU... UMMM...

DO I WHAT?

DO YOU... UMM... DO YOU... UMMM... DO YOU... UMMM... DO YOU... UMMM... DO YOU... UM... DO YOU... UMMM...

ZOE, IF YOU CAN'T ASK ME THE QUESTION, I CAN'T GIVE YOU AN ANSWER.

WELL... DOES DADDY WANT TEA OR WATER WITH DINNER?

HE CAN'T GIVE ME AN ANSWER.

BABY BLUES®

RICK KIRKMAN / JERRY SCOTT BY

47

I'M DONE!

WAIT! AREN'T YOU GOING TO FINISH YOUR LUNCH?

YOU LEFT THREE-FOURTHS OF YOUR HOTDOG, MOST OF YOUR POTATO SALAD, AND DIDN'T EVEN **TOUCH** YOUR GREEN BEANS!

YOU CAN HAVE IT.

PAT PAT

THAT'S THE TROUBLE WITH LEFTOVERS... THEY EITHER GO TO WASTE, OR GO TO WAIST.

KIRKMAN & SCOTT

LOOK AT THAT! I'LL BET IT WON'T BE LONG UNTIL HAMMIE STARTS PULLING HIMSELF UP ON THINGS.

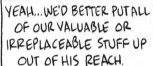
YEAH... WE'D BETTER PUT ALL OF OUR VALUABLE OR IRREPLACEABLE STUFF UP OUT OF HIS REACH.

KIRKMAN & SCOTT

WELL... **THAT** WAS EASY!

IF NOT DEPRESSING.

I GOTS A QUEXTION.

YOU MEAN, "I **HAVE** A QUESTION."

I **HAVE** A QUEXTION.

QUESTION. Kweś·chən.

QUEXTION.

OKAY. NEVER MIND... WE'LL WORK ON THAT LATER. WHAT'S YOUR QUESTION?

HOW DO YOU SAY "QUEXTION"?

KIRKMAN & SCOTT

48

BABY BLUES®

RICK KIRKMAN / JERRY SCOTT BY

50

BABY BLUES

BY RICK KIRKMAN / JERRY SCOTT

WHAT'S DAT?

PAT PAT

IT'S A CLOTH DIAPER... SEE? I PUT IT ON MY SHOULDER WHEN I'M BURPING HAMMIE.

THAT WAY, IF HE SPITS UP IT WON'T GET ALL OVER MY—

BLORP!

—SHIRT.

DIDN'T WORK.

KIRKMAN & SCOTT

IT'S MORNINGTIME, DADDY! GET UP!

LET'S PWAY! LET'S EAT BWEAKFAST! LET'S WATCH TV! LET'S PAINT!

ZIP!

KIRKMAN & SCOTT

DON'T YOU WISH YOU HAD THAT MUCH ENERGY FIRST THING IN THE MORNING?

IT'S MORNING??

LET'S SEE THAT FIRST TOOTH OF YOURS, BIG FELLA!

COME ON... OPEN UP! OPEN! OPEN!

I KNOW HOW YOU CAN MAKE HIM OPEN HIS MOUTH... DO WHAT MOMMY DOES!

WHAT'S THAT?

SHOW HIM YOUR NIPPLE.

KIRKMAN & SCOTT

YOU KNOW WHAT'S SO GREAT ABOUT KIDS? THEIR INNOCENCE.

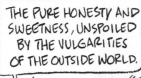

THE PURE HONESTY AND SWEETNESS, UNSPOILED BY THE VULGARITIES OF THE OUTSIDE WORLD.

SEEYA, BUTTHEAD.

KIRKMAN & SCOTT

WELL, UNSPOILED BY **MOST** OF THE VULGARITIES OF THE OUTSIDE WORLD.

WHERE DID YOU HEAR THAT **WORD**???

WHAT ARE YOU THINKING ABOUT?

THE KIDS, TAXES, EDUCATION. BIRTHDAY PARTIES, TONIGHT'S DINNER, TOMORROW NIGHT'S DINNER. NEXT THANKSGIVING. CHRISTMAS. GRAY HAIR. HEALTH INSURANCE. MY CLOTHES. LOSING WEIGHT. NEW FURNITURE. AND THE FUDGE BROWNIES I MADE FOR DESSERT.

WHAT ARE **YOU** THINKING ABOUT?

THE FUDGE BROWNIES.

KIRKMAN & SCOTT

SHOW MOMMY YOUR PRETTY NEW TOOTH, HAMMIE!

COME ON! SMILE! SMILE! SMILE!

F L A S H

YOU FINALLY GOT A PICTURE OF THE TOOTH? HOW DID IT COME OUT?

GREAT!

I GOT THE PICTURE I WANTED, PLUS AN IDEA FOR NEXT HALLOWEEN'S JACK-O'-LANTERN.

KIRKMAN & SCOTT

54

BABY BLUES®

RICK KIRKMAN / BY JERRY SCOTT

I HAFTA GO POTTY!

OKAY... DO YOU NEED ME TO HELP YOU GET UNDRESSED?

NO.

DO YOU WANT ME TO HELP YOU GET DRESSED AFTERWARDS?

DO YOU WANT ME TO GO WITH YOU?

NO.

NO.

DO YOU WANT ME TO WAIT OUTSIDE THE DOOR?

NO.

THEN WHAT DO YOU WANT ME TO DO??

CLAP WHEN I'M DONE.

KNOCK IT OFF, ZOE! SOMETIMES YOU ACT JUST LIKE YOUR MOTHER!

...WHICH IS A VERY NICE THING! YESSIREE! GOOD GIRL!

PAT! PAT!

OH! HI, DEAR!

WHAT DOES "CRETIN" MEAN?

IT'S JUST YOUR MOMMY'S WAY OF SAYING THANKS.

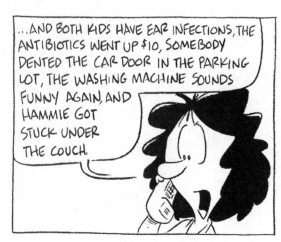

...AND BOTH KIDS HAVE EAR INFECTIONS, THE ANTIBIOTICS WENT UP $10, SOMEBODY DENTED THE CAR DOOR IN THE PARKING LOT, THE WASHING MACHINE SOUNDS FUNNY AGAIN, AND HAMMIE GOT STUCK UNDER THE COUCH.

WOW!

REMEMBER WHEN I WOULD CALL YOU TO ASK WHAT WAS NEW AND YOU'D SAY "NOTHING"?

BARELY.

BABY BLUES®

BY RICK KIRKMAN / JERRY SCOTT

WHERE WOULD I FIND THE MEASURING SPOONS?

PROBABLY THE SAME PLACE YOU'D FIND ALL THE OTHER KITCHEN UTENSILS.

OH YEAH. WHAT WAS I THINKING?

DO YOU NEED ANYTHING WHILE I'M OUT HERE?

I THINK IT'S TIME WE FOUND A REGULAR BABY SITTER SO THAT THE KIDS WILL FEEL MORE COMFORTABLE WHEN WE GO OUT.

OKAY.

SOMEONE WE TRUST. SOMEONE WE CAN COUNT ON. SOMEONE THE KIDS LIKE.

BAM!

SOMEONE WHO COULD SURVIVE...

GOOD LUCK.

HERE IT IS...

WANTED: Intelligent, pragmatic individual to fill important position.

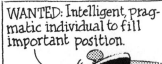

Applicant should be experienced, enthusiastic, creative, and able to handle difficult management decisions. Compensation negotiable. Transportation provided. References required.

SO, DO YOU THINK WE'LL GET ANY CALLS?

ARE WE LOOKING FOR A CEO OR A BABY SITTER?

...AND FINALLY, IF YOU WERE BABY-SITTING FOR US, WHAT WOULD YOU DO IF ONE OF THE KIDS WOULDN'T STOP CRYING?

WELL, OF COURSE, FIRST I'D TRY TO FIND THE REASON FOR THE CRYING AND REMEDY THE PROBLEM...

...AND IF THAT WASN'T POSSIBLE, I THINK I'D CALL YOU AND REPORT THE SITUATION PROMPTLY.

GOOD ANSWER. WELL, THANK YOU FOR COMING...WE'LL BE IN TOUCH.

SO YOU DIDN'T LIKE THAT ONE EITHER?

WHAT MAKES YOU SAY THAT?

HI, WHAT CAN I DO FOR YOU?

I'M HERE TO INTERVIEW FOR THE BABY-SITTING JOB.

OH... HA! HA! THERE MUST BE SOME MISTAKE... WE WERE LOOKING FOR SOMEONE A LITTLE MORE EXP—

I HAVE SIX BROTHERS AND SISTERS, I'VE BEEN CHANGING DIAPERS SINCE I WAS THREE, AND I'LL WORK FOR TWO BUCKS AN HOUR.

WELL, THAT'S VERY IMPRESSIVE, BUT I...

PLUS, I CAN FIX COMPUTERS.

HONEY, THERE'S SOMEONE I'D ♪ LIKE YOU TO MEET... ♪

KIRKMAN & SCOTT

EXCUSE US, KIKI... WE'LL BE RIGHT BACK.

OKAY.

YOU CAN'T BE SERIOUS! SHE'S SO YOUNG!

I KNOW, BUT SHE SEEMS LIKE SHE'D BE A REALLY GOOD BABY SITTER! LET'S GIVE HER A—

HI. I HOPE YOU DON'T MIND, BUT IT'S LATE, SO I PUT BOTH KIDS IN THEIR JAMMIES, BRUSHED THEIR TEETH, AND PUT THEM TO BED. IF YOU NEED ME, I'LL BE PICKING UP THEIR TOYS IN THE LIVING ROOM.

— CHANCE.

GIVE HER A CHANCE?? LET'S ADOPT HER!

I THINK YOU ARE A VERY PRETTY GIRL!

FROZEN FOOD

WHAT DO YOU SAY TO THE LADY, ZOE?

I THINK YOU HAVE A REALLY FAT BOTTOM.

YOU KNOW HOW I SAID YOU SHOULD ALWAYS TELL THE TRUTH? WELL, I'VE CHANGED MY MIND.

KIRKMAN & SCOTT

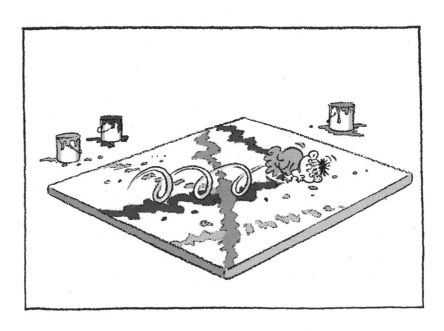

...FIVE... SIX... SEVEN... EIGHT... NINE... TEN! WEADY OR NOT, HERE I COME!

DADDY? DADDY?

DADDYYYY!

I'M RIGHT HERE, ZOE! IT'S OKAY!

YOU'RE KIND OF NEW TO THIS GAME, AREN'T YOU?

YOU PLAY WITH ME, MOMMY... HE'S TOO EASY.

THAT'S A PACIFIER. THEY'RE FOR BABIES.

UH-HUH.

THUP! THUP! THUP!

HAMMIE IS A BABY, SO HE HAS A PACIFIER. I'M NOT A BABY. I'M A **BIG** GIRL. I DON'T HAVE A PACIFIER ANYMORE. PACIFIERS ARE FOR BABIES.

RIGHT.

THUP! THUP! THUP! THUP!

WAAAA-AAAA-AA!

BABY!

BOYS ARE DOCTORS AN' GIRLS ARE CHEER-LEADERS.

WHAT?? NO! NO! NO! NO! NO!

GIRLS CAN BE DOCTORS, TOO, ZOE! THEY CAN ALSO BE LAWYERS, PHARMACISTS, TEACHERS, FIREFIGHTERS, ARTISTS, WRITERS, POLICE OFFICERS...

GIRLS CAN BE **WHATEVER** THEY WANT!

WHAT CAN BOYS BE?

USUALLY WHATEVER GIRLS WANT THEM TO BE.

DON'T COMPLICATE THIS, OKAY?

WHY ARE YOU CHANGING HAMMIE'S DIAPER?

THAT'S A SILLY QUESTION... BECAUSE HE'S A BABY AND HE STILL WETS HIMSELF!

NO... I MEAN, WHY ARE **YOU** CHANGING HIM AN' NOT **DADDY**?

CAN SOMEBODY TELL ME WHY I SUDDENLY HAVE A MOIST NAKED BABY IN MY LAP?

I SAID COME HERE SO I CAN BRUSH YOUR HAIR!

NOOO!

JUST HOLD STILL!

STOP TWISTING!

NO!

OWW! LEMME GO!

THERE! I GUESS THAT'LL HAVE TO DO.

WAAAA!

YOU MISSED A SPOT.

KIRKMAN & SCOTT

HA! HA! HA! LOOK AT THIS PICTURE OF ME WHEN I WAS PREGNANT WITH HAMMIE!

WHAT A TUBB-O! WHAT A HEIFER! MOOOOOOOO!

THIS IS WHERE I SAY SOMETHING LIKE, "DON'T BE SILLY, DEAR. YOU'RE BEAUTIFUL WHEN YOU'RE PREGNANT." RIGHT?

YOU'RE CATCHING ON.

KIRKMAN & SCOTT

BABY BLUES®

BY RICK KIRKMAN / JERRY SCOTT

HAPPY EASTER, DADDY!

¡GASP! THAT'S RIGHT! IT'S EASTER!

OH BOY! LET'S GO SEE IF THE EASTER BUNNY LEFT US SOME PRESENTS UNDER THE EASTER TREE!

NO! THAT'S CHRISTMUS!

OH YEAH... I FORGOT. EASTER IS WHEN WE DRESS UP IN RABBIT COSTUMES AND GO EASTER-TREATING AROUND THE NEIGHBORHOOD AND GET CANDY.

DADDY! DAT'S HALLOWEEN!

IT IS? OOPS! MY MISTAKE!

NOW I REMEMBER...EASTER IS THE HOLIDAY WHEN MOM COOKS THE EASTER BUNNY AND WE SIT AROUND AND WATCH FOOTBALL ON TV.

EEEEEEEEEE!

WAAAAAAAAAAA!

IT WAS A JOKE!

JUST FOR THAT, YOU'RE SITTING IN THE FRONT PEW AT CHURCH.

DO YOU REALIZE THAT WE'RE GOING TO HAVE TWO KIDS IN COLLEGE AT THE SAME TIME?

YUP.

HOW ARE WE GOING TO DO IT? HOW WILL WE AFFORD IT?

EASY...

...YOU PUT AWAY A LITTLE MONEY EACH MONTH WHILE THE KIDS ARE GROWING UP, AND WHEN THEY'RE READY FOR COLLEGE...

...YOU PANIC.

THANKS. I FEEL MUCH BETTER NOW.

LOOK! HAMMIE IS WALKING!

¡GRUNT! LOOK! HAMMIE IS FLYING!

LOOK! HAMMIE IS READING!

CHOMP!

WAAAAAA!

LOOK! HAMMIE IS DEFENDING HIMSELF!

WHAK!

OW!

THONK!

OUUCH!

GOTCHA!

OOOOF!

THUD!

TIME FOR BED...DADDY'S TIRED.

BLESS YOU.

66

BABY BLUES

BY RICK KIRKMAN / JERRY SCOTT

ZOE! THESE TOYS OF YOURS ARE **STILL** IN THE MIDDLE OF THE LIVING ROOM FLOOR!

COME AND PICK THIS STUFF UP RIGHT NOW!

I MEAN IT! DO YOU HEAR ME??

OKAY! I'M COMING!

THAT'S MORE LIKE IT! YOU'RE A BIG GIRL NOW, AND YOU'RE OLD ENOUGH TO LISTEN TO MOMMY.

I SHOULDN'T HAVE TO SCREAM AT YOU MORE THAN ONCE.

CAN I HELP YOU FIX SOMETHING, DADDY?

HUH? UH... OKAY, SURE!

HERE YOU GO... HAVE A WRENCH.

I DON'T THINK YOU CAN DO MUCH DAMAGE WITH—

—THAT.

WHAT ELSE CAN I FIX?

WHEN I GWOW UP, I'M GONNA BE A FIREFIGHTER!

THAT'S GREAT, ZOE!

AN' A DOCTOR!

AN' A BALLERINA!

TERRIFIC!

WONDERFUL!

ARE YOU IMPRESSED?

I'M TRYING TO PICTURE WHAT SHE'S GOING TO WEAR TO WORK.

HEY!

WHAT?

IT'S 6 A.M. AND I DON'T REMEMBER GETTING UP ONCE WITH THE KIDS LAST NIGHT!

DO YOU REALIZE WHAT THIS MEANS??

I SURE DO!

IT MEANS IT'S YOUR TURN TONIGHT!

68

SLAM!

I THINK I'LL GO CLEAN THE GUTTERS, HOSE DOWN THE DRIVE-WAY, AND WASH THE CARS.

WOW! THAT'S PRETTY AMBITIOUS!

IT'S EITHER THAT OR MATCH UP A DRYERFUL OF BABY SOCKS.

HEY! WAIT A MINUTE!

KIRKMAN & SCOTT

ON SECOND THOUGHT, MAYBE HAMMIE COULD SKIP HIS NAP TODAY...

WIMP.

KIRKMAN & SCOTT

RING!

HELLO? HELLO?

RING!

KIRKMAN & SCOTT

HELLO? HELLO? HELLOOOO!!!

RING! RING!

YOU HAVE TO PICK IT UP FIRST.

OH.

RING!

Baby Blues®

BY
RICK KIRKMAN / JERRY SCOTT

BUNNY CALLED.

WHAT DID SHE WANT?

SOMETHING ABOUT WANTING TO GIVE YOU AN ARTICLE ON HOW TO MAKE FESTIVE WREATHS OUT OF OLD ORANGE JUICE CANS, CEREAL BOXES AND EGG SHELLS.

JUST STAY OUT OF OUR GARBAGE CAN, OKAY??

TO SOME PEOPLE RECYCLING IS NOT JUST A DUTY... IT'S AN OBSESSION.

KIRKMAN & SCOTT

I THINK ZOE IS GETTING BORED WITH STAYING HOME ALL DAY.

WHAT SHOULD WE DO... GIVE HER A SET OF KEYS TO THE CAR?

:SIGH:

NO, I THINK WE SHOULD PUT HER IN PRESCHOOL FOR A COUPLE OF MORNINGS A WEEK.

YOU DO??

YES! SHE WOULD BE OUT AMONG OTHER PEOPLE, LEARNING NEW STUFF... JUST THINK OF ALL THE THINGS SHE COULD PICK UP OUT THERE!

FORGET IT.

WHY??

BECAUSE OF ALL THE THINGS SHE COULD PICK UP OUT THERE!

ZOE, HOW WOULD YOU LIKE TO GO TO PRESCHOOL?

NO.

LET ME TRY.

GUESS WHAT, ZOE?... YOU GET TO GO TO PRESCHOOL!

NO!

I'VE GOT IT... I'VE GOT IT...

IF YOU'RE REALLY, REALLY GOOD, MOMMY AND DADDY WILL LET YOU GO TO PRESCHOOL!

NO!

:SIGH:

KIRKMAN & SCOTT

WELL, IT WOULD HAVE BEEN PRETTY EXPENSIVE ANYWAY...

I WANNA GO! I WANNA GO!

DARRYL! GUESS WHAT?... I FOUND THE **PERFECT** PRESCHOOL FOR ZOE.

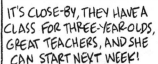

IT'S CLOSE-BY, THEY HAVE A CLASS FOR THREE-YEAR-OLDS, GREAT TEACHERS, AND SHE CAN START NEXT WEEK!

THERE'S ONLY ONE PROBLEM. IT'S THE BEST PRESCHOOL IN THE CITY, AND THEY THINK ZOE HAS THE PERFECT QUALIFICATIONS.

SO WHAT'S THE PROBLEM?

THEY'RE NOT SURE **WE** DO.

KIRKMAN & SCOTT

MR. AND MRS. MacPHERSON, I'M GEOFFREY ENGLE, THE HEADMASTER HERE AT REDFIELD PRESCHOOL.

REDFIELD IS THE FINEST PRESCHOOL IN THE STATE, WINNER OF THE PRESTIGIOUS "EDUCATOR'S TROPHY" THREE YEARS RUNNING, AND THIS YEAR'S RECIPIENT OF THE COVETED "PLATINUM CRAYON AWARD."

MY!

WOW!

NOW, HOW MAY I HELP YOU?

WE'D LIKE TO ENROLL OUR DAUGHTER HERE.

WONDERFUL! WHEN WILL SHE BE BORN?

I SMELL **WAITING** LIST.

KIRKMAN & SCOTT

WELL, WE FOUND A REALLY GOOD PRESCHOOL FOR ZOE TODAY.

HEY, THAT'S GREAT!

MY SCHOOL!

SHE STARTS NEXT WEEK: TUESDAYS AND THURSDAYS, NINE TO ELEVEN-THIRTY.

TERRIFIC!

SCHOOL! SCHOOL! SCHOOL!

GREAT!

WONDERFUL!

EXCITING!

A MILESTONE!

YOU BET!

YESSIREE!

WAAAAAA!

KIRKMAN & SCOTT

IT'S THREE O'CLOCK IN THE MORNING, ZOE... WHAT'S THE MATTER??

DERE'S SOMETHING SCARY UNDER MY BED!

HE'S REALLY UNDER THERE! LOOK!

WOULD YOU MIND?

OKAY... SURE, WHAT THE HECK, I'LL TAKE A—

AIEEEEEE!

MONSTER??

HUMONGOUS DUST BUNNY.

SEE?

KIRKMAN & SCOTT

I MADE AN APPOINTMENT FOR ZOE TO HAVE HER HAIR CUT BEFORE SHE GOES TO PRESCHOOL.

REALLY? AT THE BEAUTY SHOP!

YEAH. IT'LL BE FUN. WE CAN TAKE SOME "BEFORE" AND "AFTER" PICTURES.

OF HER, OR US?

KIRKMAN & SCOTT

THIS IS A BEAUTY SHOP, ZOE.

WAAAAA!

AND THIS IS RACHELA... SHE'S GOING TO CUT YOUR HAIR.

WAAAAAA!

YOU GET TO SIT IN THIS BIG CHAIR THAT GOES UP AND DOWN IN FRONT OF A BIG MIRROR!

KIRKMAN & SCOTT

AND WHEN YOU'RE FINISHED, THERE WILL BE A TREAT!

WAAAAA!

FOR HER, OR ME?

WAAAAAAAAAAAAA!WAAAAAAAAAA!WAAAAAAAAAAAAAAAAAAAA!WAAAAAAAAAA!

HOW WOULD YOU LIKE ME TO CUT IT?
YES! THAT SOUNDS FINE!

HOW SHORT SHOULD IT BE?
YES, SHE JUST TURNED THREE.

JUST TELL ME THE STYLE!
OKAY, LET'S ALL SMILE!

AREN'T YOU GOING TO ASK ME HOW I WANT IT CUT?
:SIGH:

ALL FINISHED! WHAT DO YOU THINK?
IT'S CUTE! IT'S ADORABLE! IT'S HER!
SNIF!

THANKS AGAIN! BYE!
Salon

IS SHE STILL LOOKING?
NOPE. SHE'S GONE.

COMB! BRUSH! COMB! BRUSH!

ZOE, I WANT YOU TO—

SHHH! QUIET, DADDY! MY BABY IS SLEEPING!
BUT... I...

LOOK WHAT YOU DID! YOU WOKE HER UP! OH DEAR! THAT DOES IT!

I THOUGHT YOU WERE GOING TO MAKE ZOE PICK UP HER TOYS...
IT'S A LONG STORY...

KIRKMAN & SCOTT

BABY BLUES

RICK KIRKMAN / JERRY SCOTT

OUR LITTLE GIRL'S FIRST DAY OF PRESCHOOL...

ARE YOU EXCITED?

ARE YOU READY?

ARE YOU AFRAID?

NO.

NO.

YES.

ACTUALLY, I WAS TALKING TO ZOE.

CAN WE GO NOW?

KIRKMAN & SCOTT

HAPPY HANDS PRESCHOOL

SPRING SING

KIRKMAN & SCOTT

NOW THAT ZOE IS OFFICIALLY IN PRESCHOOL, I HAVE TO FIGURE OUT WHAT TO DO WITH MY MORNINGS.

IF I ADD THE TIME IT TAKES ME TO DRIVE HOME AND BACK, AND THE TIME IT TAKES ME TO GET HAMMIE IN AND OUT OF THE CAR SEAT...

...AND I SUBTRACT THAT FROM THE HOURS ZOE IS IN SCHOOL, IT LEAVES ME EXACTLY...

...NOTHING.

SCREECH!

HAPPY HANDS PRESCHOOL

KIRKMAN & SCOTT

BABY BLUES®

BY RICK KIRKMAN / JERRY SCOTT

CHINKITTY-CLINK! CHINKITTY-CLINK! CHINKITTY-CLINK!

WHAT THE-?

OH GOOD! YOU'RE HOME! DINNER IS IN THE OVEN...WE'LL BE BACK BY EIGHT O'CLOCK.

DADDY!

THE VAN IS MAKING A RATTLE BUT I DON'T THINK IT'S SERIOUS.

OKAY... BYE!

WAA-WAAAAA!

MO-O-MMY! HAMMIE TOUCHED ME!!

WHAT RATTLE?

KIRKMAN & SCOTT

BONK!

HI, ZOE! HOW WAS YOUR FIRST DAY OF PRESCHOOL?

GREAT. THIS IS TRENT. HE'S MY NEW FRIEND.

WELL, HI THERE, TRENT. IT'S NICE TO MEET YOU! WHAT CUTE FRECKLES YOU HAVE.

POP! POP! POP!

POP! POP! POP! POP! POP! POP! POP! POP! POP! POP! POP!

THEY ARE FRECKLES, AREN'T THEY, TRENT?

CHICKEN-POX!!!

POP! POP! POP! POP! POP! POP!

I CAN'T BELIEVE THAT ZOE WAS EXPOSED TO CHICKENPOX ON HER VERY FIRST DAY OF PRESCHOOL!

WHAT'S CHIPPEN POPS?

CHICKEN-POX. IT'S A DISEASE THAT KIDS GET.

WHAT'S A DIZEEZE?

A DISEASE IS A SICKNESS. YOU MIGHT GET SICK IN A WEEK OR SO BECAUSE YOU PLAYED WITH TRENT.

OH.

PLAYING WITH BOYS WILL MAKE ME SICK?

YES. REMEMBER THAT.

YOU'RE NOT HELPING HERE!

ARE YOU GUYS PLAYING CATCH?

HUH?

CATCH: WHEN YOU THROW THE BALL TO EACH OTHER AND YOU CATCH IT, IT'S CALLED "CATCH."

BONK!

KIRKMAN & SCOTT

THEN THAT'S NOT WHAT WE'RE PLAYING.

DO YOU EVER WONDER IF WE'RE PROVIDING THE KIDS WITH A GOOD CHILDHOOD?

LET'S SEE...THEIR OWN ROOMS, GOBS OF TOYS, STACKS OF BOOKS AND VIDEOS, ACCESS TO A COLOR TV AND A VCR, A PRIVATE BATHROOM, RECREATIONAL ACTIVITIES, A CAR AND DRIVER TO TAKE THEM ANYWHERE THEY NEED TO GO...

THIS ISN'T CHILDHOOD... IT'S A RESORT!

KIRKMAN & SCOTT

THAT OUGHT TO DO IT, HAM.

HAM? NO, THIS IS DAIRY... THE MEAT COUNTER IS DOWN THERE.

NO... HE'S HAM. THAT'S HIS NAME!

NAMING A CHILD AFTER A PORK PRODUCT... TALK ABOUT WEIRDOS.

HAM IS SHORT FOR HAMISH! GET IT? HAM? HAM?

THIS IS THE DAIRY CASE... THE MEAT COUNTER IS DOWN THERE.

SIGH!

KIRKMAN & SCOTT

YOLANDA?
IT'S WANDA.

I DON'T THINK YOU WANT KEESHA TO COME OVER TODAY... ZOE HAS CHICKENPOX.

KNOCK!
KNOCK!
KNOCK!

HANG ON... SOMEBODY IS AT THE DOOR.

YOLANDA...

COUGH UP SOME GERMS! WE WANT TO GET IT OVER WITH.

KIRKMAN & SCOTT

THAT MAKES ALMOST EVERY MOTHER IN THE NEIGHBORHOOD WHO HAS BROUGHT HER KID TO BE EXPOSED TO ZOE'S CHICKENPOX.

ALMOST?

YEAH, EVERY ONE BUT BUNNY, NEXT DOOR.

OH, OF COURSE! A CASE OF CHICKENPOX MIGHT UPSET HER PERFECT LIFE!

OKAY, ZOE... SNEEZE!

KIRKMAN & SCOTT

HI, HONEY... HOW ARE THE KIDS DOING?

JUST PEACHY.

THEIR CHICKENPOX IS ITCHING LIKE CRAZY, THEY'RE BORED, AND THE VCR JUST STOPPED WORKING.

POOR LITTLE KIDS...

IS THERE ANYTHING THAT I CAN PICK UP ON THE WAY HOME THAT WOULD HELP?

A QUART OF RUM AND TWO TICKETS TO HAWAII.

I MEANT FOR THE KIDS.

KIRKMAN & SCOTT

...I READ SOMEWHERE THAT IF YOU FASTEN THE BRACKET—

DADDY! DADDY! DADDY!

ZOE, DADDY IS ON THE PHONE! IT'S NOT POLITE TO INTERRUPT.

OH.

ANYWAY, IF YOU FASTEN THE BRACKET TO THE—

DADDY! DADDY! DADDY!

WHAT DOES "INTERRUPT" MEAN?

WAKE UP, ZOE! HURRY! WE HAVE TO GET READY FOR PRESCHOOL!

ZZZZ

EAT! GIVE ME YOUR FOOT! POINT YOUR TOES! CHEW! SWALLOW!

TUCK YOUR SHIRT IN! DON'T RUN! BE CAREFUL! HAVE FUN! I LOVE YOU!

I USED TO THINK I WAS BUSY... THEN I BECAME THE MOTHER OF A PRESCHOOLER!

ROOKIE, EH?

I'M THE DOCTOR AN' YOU BE THE SICK GUY.

OKAY.

SAY "AHH."

AHHHHHHH...

AHHHHHH—

ZOE! HOW MANY TIMES HAVE I TOLD YOU TO STOP TAKING THAT FILTHY STICK OUT OF THE TRASH??

AHHHHHHHHH...

87

HANG ON! I'M COMING TO RESCUE YOU!

:GRUNT!: OOF! ERF! AARRGH!

AACK! UNFF! MMMAARGH!

I DON'T THINK HAMMIE WANTS TO BE RESCUED RIGHT THIS MINUTE, ZOE.

TOO BAD.

KIRKMAN & SCOTT

I WAS THINKING ABOUT SOMETHING IMPORTANT TODAY.

WHAT WAS IT?

I DON'T REMEMBER.

WELL, WAS IT ABOUT MONEY?

THE KIDS?

US? OUR PARENTS?

I DON'T KNOW.

BEATS ME.

I HAVE NO IDEA.

YOU STAY HOME RAISING KIDS FOR THREE YEARS AND WE'LL SEE HOW GOOD YOUR MEMORY IS!

KIRKMAN & SCOTT

GNAW! GNAW! GNAW! GNAW!

DO YOU HEAR SOMETHING?

YEAH.

GNAW! GNAW! GNAW! GNAW!

IT SOUNDS LIKE CHEWING OR SOMETHING.

YOU DON'T SUPPOSE IT'S TERMITES, DO YOU?

GNAW! GNAW! GNAW! GNAW!

I DON'T KNOW... I'M NOT SURE WHERE IT'S—

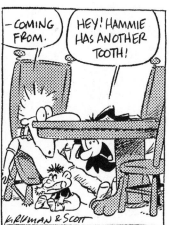

—COMING FROM.

HEY! HAMMIE HAS ANOTHER TOOTH!

KIRKMAN & SCOTT

BABY BLUES®

BY RICK KIRKMAN / JERRY SCOTT

MOMMY!

HI, ZOE!

HOW WAS PRESCHOOL TODAY?

I DUNNO.

WELL, WHAT DID YOU **DO**?

I DUNNO.

DID YOU HEAR STORIES?

I DUNNO.

DID YOU DRAW PICTURES?

I DUNNO.

DID YOU PLAY ON THE SLIDE?

I DUNNO.

PRESCHOOL CAUSES AMNESIA.

KIRKMAN & SCOTT

BOOGERNOSE!

ZOE!

WE DON'T USE LANGUAGE LIKE THAT AROUND HERE.

OH.

I WANT YOU TO TELL HAMMIE YOU'RE SORRY, AND PROMISE ME YOU'LL NEVER USE THAT WORD AGAIN.

I'M SORRY, I PROMISE.

HONESTLY! I DON'T KNOW WHERE SHE PICKS UP ALL THAT STUFF!

HIYA, BOOGERNOSE!

KIRKMAN & SCOTT

BPTH MNGL.

HAMMIE WANTS HIS TEDDY BEAR.

OKAY...

ONGL NFIG.

HAMMIE SAYS HE WOULD LIKE THAT TRUCK, TOO.

WOW! YOU REALLY UNDERSTAND HIM?

MMPTH GMM MAA!

HAMMIE SAYS HE WANTS HIS PACIFIER.

A TRANSLATOR! THIS IS GREAT!

MERPP.

AN' HE THINKS YOU SHOULD GIVE ME FIVE COOKIES.

NICE TRY.

KIRKMAN & SCOTT

BABY BLUES®

BY RICK KIRKMAN / JERRY SCOTT

WHAT ARE THOSE THINGS THE KIDS ARE PLAYING WITH, BUNNY?

OH! YOU HAVEN'T SEEN THOSE?

IT'S A BRAND-NEW TOY CONCEPT FROM SWITZERLAND... EVERYBODY HAS THEM!

CLICK! CLICK!

THEY DO?

SURE! SEE? THEY'RE TOTALLY NON-VIOLENT, EDUCATIONAL, EARTH-FRIENDLY, UNISEX TOYS DESIGNED TO PROMOTE COOPERATIVE PLAY AMONG CHILDREN.

YOU'RE THE ONLY PERSON I KNOW WHO HASN'T HEARD ABOUT THEM!

I AM?

WOULD YOU LIKE TO SEE THE BROCHURE?

OKAY... SURE... I GUESS SO... THAT WOULD BE GREAT.

CLICK!

CLICK!

POW! BANG-BANG! GOTCHA!

POW! POW! POW! AAAAAGH!

NEVER MIND!

POW! POW! GOTCHA!

ZOE, WHAT WERE YOU JUST DOING?

SHOOTIN' A GUN.

WHERE DID YOU LEARN ABOUT GUNS?

TOBY TAUGHT ME AT SCHOOL! BANG! BANG!

!SIGH!

I GUESS THERE'S MORE TO EDUCATION THAN WHAT YOU GET FROM A TEACHER...

AND, HE KNOWS LOTS OF FUNNY NAMES FOR OUR BODY PARTS!

KIRKMAN & SCOTT

BRAAAP!

SAY "EXCUSE ME," ZOE.

WHY?

BECAUSE YOU JUST DID SOMETHING IMPOLITE. WHEN YOU DO SOMETHING IMPOLITE, YOU SHOULD SAY "EXCUSE ME."

EVERY TIME?

EVERY TIME.

S'CUSE ME. S'CUSE ME. S'CUSE ME. S'CUSE ME. S'CUSE ME.

OR YOU COULD TRY NOT TO DO IT AT ALL!

KIRKMAN & SCOTT

YESTERDAY WAS THE FIRST OF JUNE, ZOE. CAN YOU SAY "JUNE"?

JOOON.

JUNE RHYMES WITH MOON. AND SPOON, AND BALLOON!

THAT'S FUN TO SAY, ISN'T IT? JUNE... MOON... SPOON... BALLOON...

KIRKMAN & SCOTT

BABOON... LOON... CARTOON... SPITTOON...

JUST HOW MANY MISTER ROGERS SHOWS HAS MOMMY BEEN WATCHING?

A LOT.

WAAAA AAAAA!

NOW YOU SIT THERE FOR TWO MINUTES AND THINK ABOUT CHANGING YOUR BEHAVIOR, YOUNG LADY!

WAAAAAAAA!

WAAAAAAA!

WHY ONLY TWO MINUTES?

THAT'S ALL I CAN STAND.

SHRIEK! HA! HA! HA! HA! HA!

HA! HA! HA! HA! HA! HA!

WHAT IN THE WORLD IS SO FUNNY?

GIGGLE! GASP! DADDY GIGGLE! IS WEARING SNORT! CLOWN PANTIES!!! HA! HA! HA! HA!

KIRKMAN & SCOTT

AND YOU WONDER WHY I LIKE BRIEFS BETTER THAN BOXERS...

SHRIEK! SEE???

LOOK, MOMMY AN' DADDY! I DRESSED MYSELF!

OH!

YOU SURE DID!

IS THAT WHAT YOU WANT TO WEAR TO SCHOOL?

UH-HUH.

WHAT DO YOU THINK?

I DON'T KNOW WHETHER TO HURT HER PRIDE OR SWALLOW MINE.

I LOOK GOOD!

KIRKMAN & SCOTT

BABY BLUES®

BY RICK KIRKMAN / JERRY SCOTT

THE MALE SEA HORSE HAS A KANGAROO-LIKE POUCH ON ITS ABDOMEN.

THE FEMALE LAYS HER EGGS IN THE MALE'S POUCH, WHERE THEY REMAIN UNTIL THEY HATCH.

AT THAT TIME, THE MALE CONTORTS HIS BODY AND EXPELS THE YOUNG THROUGH THE TINY OPENING IN THE POUCH.

DO YOU UNDERSTAND, ZOE? THE **DADDY** SEA HORSE HAS THE BABIES INSTEAD OF THE **MOMMY**!

WOW!

{SIGH!} I WONDER IF HE TAKES OUT THE TRASH AND LEAVES THE TOILET SEAT DOWN, TOO...?

NO MORE VIDEOS FOR FATHER'S DAY, OKAY? NEXT YEAR I WANT **TOOLS!**

RiiiNG!

H'LO? WHO IS IT, PLEASE?

OH, HI AUNT RHONDA! GOOD... GOOD... UH-HUH... UH-HUH... UH-HUH... YES...

KIRKMAN & SCOTT

IS YOUR MOMMY THERE?

JUST ABOUT.

YOU'RE ¿PANT! SUPPOSED TO ¿WHEEZE!¿ GIVE ME A HEAD START ¿GASP!¿ REMEMBER?

SO, ZOE, WHAT DID YOU DO AT PRESCHOOL TODAY?

WELL, WE ALL SAT IN OUR PLACES AND LISTENED, THEN WE WENT HOME.

AND WHAT ELSE?

NOTHIN'.

KIRKMAN & SCOTT

WHAT'S WRONG? DOESN'T THAT SOUND LIKE A FUN DAY?

IT SOUNDS LIKE MY DAY.

¿GIGGLE!¿ ¿GIGGLE!¿

WHAT'S SO FUNNY?

¿CHUCKLE!¿ BUNNY IS ALL WEIRDED OUT BECAUSE BOGART IS PRETENDING THAT ALL OF HIS TOYS ARE GUNS!

KIRKMAN & SCOTT

¿SNORT!¿ I SHOULDN'T LAUGH, BUT IT'S JUST SO HILARIOUS!

DON'T YOU SEE THE IRONY?

ALMOST...

STICK 'EM UP!

99

DADDY, I'LL BE THE BEAUTIFUL PRINCESS AND YOU BE THE HANDSOME PRINCE.

OKAY.

HAMMIE WILL BE THE GOOD KING, THIS DOLL WILL BE THE QUEEN, AN' THESE GUYS WILL BE DOROTHY, TOTO AN' THE MUNCHKINS.

KIRKMAN & SCOTT

WHAT ABOUT MOMMY?

YEAH! WHAT WILL I BE?

SAME AS USUAL.

WHY DO I ALWAYS HAVE TO BE THE WICKED WITCH?

'CUZ YOU'RE GOOD AT IT.

THAT WAS A COMPLIMENT, RIGHT, ZOE?

SO HAMMIE DOESN'T WANT TO TAKE NAPS ANYMORE, HUH?

NOPE, THIS IS DEFINITELY A NEW PHASE HE'S IN.

WELL, HAVE YOU TRIED—

YOU NAME IT, I'VE TRIED IT.

WELL, IT'S HARD TO BELIEVE NOTHING WORKS.

TRUST ME ON THIS.

KIRKMAN & SCOTT

DING-DONG!

KIKI IS HERE!!

HI, KIKI. HOW ARE Y—

OKAY, MOMMY AN' DADDY. GO NOW...BYE!

HAMMIE IS ASLEEP... EMERGENCY NUMBERS ARE BY THE PHONE... SNACKS ARE IN THE FR—

HAVE A GOOD TIME!

GO! GO! GO!

KIRKMAN & SCOTT

IS IT POSSIBLE FOR A BABYSITTER TO BE TOO GOOD AT HER JOB?

I WISH YOU LIVED HERE INSTEAD OF MOMMY AN' DADDY.

BABY BLUES®

BY RICK KIRKMAN / JERRY SCOTT

103

!!!!!!!

NO MORE BAKED BEANS BEFORE NURSING HAMMIE.

AGREED.

KIRKMAN & SCOTT

MOMMY?

YES?

I PUT ALL OF MY TOYS AWAY AND PUT MY DIRTY CLOTHES IN THE BASKET.

GOOD.

IF IT'S OKAY WITH YOU, I'LL VACUUM THE LIVING ROOM, FINISH THE DISHES AND KNOCK OUT A COUPLE OF LOADS OF LAUNDRY BEFORE I MAKE DINNER.

WHAT'S GOING ON?

MOMMY'S GIGGLING IN HER SLEEP AGAIN.

HEE! HEE! SURE! AND WASH THE PATIO WINDOWS WHILE YOU'RE AT IT...

SO, ZOE... WHAT DID YOU DO TODAY?

I PLAYED, AND THEN I COLORED.

AND THEN I PLAYED SOME MORE, AND THEN I COLORED SOME MORE...

...PLAYED, COLORED, PLAYED, PLAYED, COLORED, PLAYED, ATE A SNACK, COLORED, COLORED, PLAYED, PLAYED, WENT POTTY, COLORED, COLORED, COLORED...

I WAS LOOKING FOR A SUMMARY RATHER THAN A MINUTE-BY-MINUTE...

THEN YOU SHOULD HAVE SAID SO.

105

Baby Blues®

by Rick Kirkman / Jerry Scott

...AND ONE SPRING DAY, THE SIX YOUNG MEERKATS CAUTIOUSLY VENTURE FROM THEIR BURROW FOR THE FIRST TIME.

AAAWW... AREN'T THEY CUTE?

THOUGH TIMID AT FIRST, SOON THE MEERKATS ROMP PLAYFULLY IN THE SUN...

CRUNCH!

YAAAAGH!

MUNCH! MUNCH! MUNCH!

...WHICH IS A BAD IDEA WHEN THERE ARE HYENAS AROUND.

THE REMOTE! GET THE REMOTE!

CLICK!

CLICK!

A HYENA JUST ATE ONE OF THE BABY MEERKATS!

DON'T WORRY... I THINK THE OTHERS ARE GOING TO BE OKAY.

AS THE HUNGRY HYENA FEASTS ON HIS KILL, THE REST OF THE MEERKATS SCRAMBLE BACK TO THE DEN, WHERE THEY WOULD BE SAFE...

THERE! SEE?

GULP! GULP! GULP!

YAAAGH!

...IF A HUNGRY PYTHON HADN'T GOTTEN THERE FIRST.

I HATE NATURE!!

WHAT KIND OF NATURE SHOW IS THIS?? ALL OF THE CUTE LITTLE BABY MEERKATS ARE BEING EATEN ALIVE!

MAYBE THEY'RE TRYING TO MAKE A POINT ABOUT SURVIVAL. LET'S GIVE IT A CHANCE.

HAVING GAINED VALUABLE KNOWLEDGE ABOUT THE DANGERS OF THEIR SURROUNDINGS, THE MEERKATS TAKE TURNS KEEPING A SHARP LOOKOUT FOR OTHER PREDATORS IN THE BUSH...

SEE? WHAT DID I TELL YOU?

...UNAWARE THAT MEERKATS ARE ALSO A FAVORITE FOOD OF HAWKS,

SNATCH!

YAAAAAGH!

THAT'S IT! TURN IT OFF! I CAN'T WATCH ANOTHER CUTE LITTLE ANIMAL GET EATEN!

I THINK IT'S ABOUT OVER, ANYWAY.

YEAH... SEE? THERE'S THE GAME WARDEN COMING THROUGH THE BUSHES TO SAVE THE LAST BABY MEERKAT.

REALLY?

WELL, AT LEAST THAT'S SOME GOOD N—

—CHOMP!

NO, WAIT... THAT WAS ANOTHER HYENA.

YAAAAGH!

ZOE, POLITE CHILDREN EAT WITH THEIR SPOONS AND FORKS.

THEY MUST NOT BE VERY HUNGRY!

SIGH!

WHAT'S WRONG, HONEY?

I PROMISED MYSELF THAT I WOULDN'T MAKE THE SAME MISTAKES WITH HAMMIE THAT I MADE WITH ZOE...

...AND FOR THE MOST PART, I HAVEN'T.

SO WHAT'S THE PROBLEM?

SIGH! I'M MAKING ALL NEW ONES.

BABY BLUES®

BY RICK KIRKMAN / JERRY SCOTT

"HAMMIE'S BOTTOM TEETH ARE REALLY GROWING IN!"

"THEY SURE ARE!"

"I THINK HE LOOKS KIND OF CUTE."

"YOU DO?"

"I THINK HE LOOKS KIND OF LIKE SARGE IN "BEETLE BAILEY.""

"DO YOU THINK WE OUGHT TO TAKE HAMMIE TO A PEDIATRIC ORTHODONTIST?"

"WHAT?? WHY?"

"WELL, YOU HAVE TO ADMIT THAT HIS BOTTOM TEETH ARE BECOMING KIND OF PROMINENT..."

"SO?? WHAT'S WRONG WITH HAVING A PROMINENT FEATURE?"

"IT JUST DOESN'T RUN IN OUR FAMILY?"

"MUCH..."

"WHINE! WHINE! WHINE!"

"WHINE! WHINE! WHINE!"

"ZOE, IF YOU DON'T STOP WHINING, I'LL GIVE YOU SOMETHING TO WHINE ABOUT!"

"HUH??"

"IT DOESN'T MAKE ANY SENSE TO ME, EITHER, BUT IT WORKED WHEN MY MOM USED TO SAY IT."

HAVE YOU NOTICED THAT WE DON'T CARRY AROUND AS MUCH STUFF FOR HAMMIE AS WE DID WITH ZOE?

NOW THAT YOU MENTION IT, THE DIAPER BAG DOES SEEM A LITTLE LIGHTER THAN IT USED TO.

IT'S WEIRD BECAUSE IT'S ALL THE SAME STUFF...DIAPERS...WIPES...EXTRA CLOTHES— OH, WAIT! I KNOW WHAT'S MISSING!

WHAT?

THE ANXIETY.

YEAH, I GUESS THERE'S ALWAYS LESS OF THAT WITH THE SECOND BABY...

·GULP!·

GUESS WHO CRAWLED IN BED WITH US LAST NIGHT?

MOM! HAMMIE IS CRYING!

WANDA, HAVE YOU SEEN MY BELT?

MOM! HAMMIE BARFED!

I'M TAKING SOME OF YOUR CASH FOR LUNCH MONEY!

MOM! I NEED MORE CEREAL!

WANDA, DID YOU PICK UP MY JACKET FROM THE DRY CLEANER?

WHAT DO YOU MEAN WE DEPEND ON YOU TOO MUCH?

DADDY, TELL MOM I SPILLED MY MILK.

Baby Blues

BY RICK KIRKMAN / JERRY SCOTT

YOU REALLY THINK THAT WE DEPEND ON YOU TOO MUCH?

LOOK AROUND!

NOT ONLY DO I DO THE COOKING, CLEANING AND ORGANIZING AROUND HERE, I'M ALSO THE MAIN PROBLEM-SOLVER!

IF THERE'S A DISASTER, CALL **MOM**! IF THERE'S AN ERRAND TO BE RUN, CALL **MOM**! IF THERE'S A MESS TO BE CLEANED UP, AN APPOINTMENT TO KEEP, OR A DECISION TO BE MADE, CALL **MOM**!

WHAT DO YOU THINK WE SHOULD DO ABOUT THAT?

ALL I'M SAYING IS THAT I NEED A LITTLE RELIEF.

GOTCHA.

I'M TIRED OF BEING IN CHARGE OF EVERYTHING AROUND THE HOUSE, AND I NEED YOU AND ZOE TO PITCH IN AND TAKE A LITTLE MORE RESPONSIBILITY.

SAY NO MORE!

WE'LL START BY EMPTYING THE DISHWASHER FOR YOU!

THANKS, GUYS... I REALLY APPRECIATE THE—

WHERE DO THESE BOWLS GO?

—EFFORT.

I CAN'T REACH THE COUNTER, SO I'LL JUST PUT THESE ON THE FLOOR, OKAY?

WHEW! THE KIDS ARE FINALLY IN BED!

YEAH.

CLICK!

THINGS ARE SO NOISY AND CHAOTIC WHEN I GET HOME FROM WORK THAT I REALLY LOOK FORWARD TO THE PART OF THE EVENING WHEN I CAN SIT AND TALK TO...

...MYSELF.

ZZZZZ

KIRKMAN & SCOTT

ZOE, CAN YOU GET ME A T-SHIRT FOR HAMMIE?

SURE.

ERF! UNNH! HOLD STILL, HAMMIE!

POP!

WHEW! HAMMIE MUST REALLY BE GROWING, ZOE! THIS T-SHIRT IS ALMOST TOO SMALL.

THAT'S FUNNY... IT FITS MY TEDDY BEAR JUST FINE.

WATCH, DADDY, WATCH!

OKAY... I'M WATCHING!

WHUMP!

WOW! THAT WAS GREAT, ZOE! GOOD JOB! 'ATTA GIRL!

ACTUALLY, SHE JUST WANTED YOU TO SEE THE FIRST PART... THE FALLING WAS AN ACCIDENT.

OH...

THANKS A LOT, DAD.

LOOK! A CALLIPIDDER!

HEH-HEH! NO, ZOE... IT'S CATERPILLAR... NOT "CALLIPIDDER!"

CATERPILLAR.

CATERPILLAR... CATERPILLAR... CATERPILLAR... CATERPILLAR...

YES! THAT'S CORRECT! ABSOLUTELY CORRECT!

...AND TOTALLY UN-CUTE.

NICE GOING, MR. WEBSTER.

KIRKMAN & SCOTT

BABY BLUES®

BY RICK KIRKMAN / JERRY SCOTT

DEPT. OF THE MORE THINGS CHANGE, THE MORE THEY STAY THE SAME:

SINCE YOU HAVE THE WEEK OFF, MAYBE WE COULD TAKE THE KIDS TO WHISTLING MONKEY COWBOY BAND LAND FOR A DAY.

WHAT??

COME ON... IT'S ONLY A FEW HOURS AWAY.

WE COULD LEAVE EARLY IN THE MORNING, SPEND THE DAY, AND DRIVE HOME THAT EVENING.

WHAT DO YOU SAY?

NOTHING THAT COULD BE REPEATED IN MIXED COMPANY.

HOW LONG HAVE WE BEEN DRIVING?

I DON'T KNOW.

HOW MANY MILES HAVE WE GONE?

I DON'T KNOW.

MOM?...

HOW MANY POTTY STOPS SO FAR?

THIS MAKES TWENTY-SIX, BUT WHO'S COUNTING?

GAS'N STUFF

THERE IT IS, EVERYBODY! WHISTLING MONKEY COWBOY BAND LAND!

FINALLY!

YAY!

OKAY... I HAVE THE PASSES AND THE CAMERA. LET'S GO IN AND HAVE SOME REAL FAMILY...

...FUN.

NICE SHORTS, FOUR-EYES!

WHEEE!

ENTRANCE

KIRKMAN & SCOTT

119

WAAAAAA!

YEAH, WELL, I CAN DO A SOMERSAULT, AND YOU CAN'T!

WHEN I GROW UP I WANNA LIVE IN A BARBIE® HOUSE AN' HAVE A BARBIE® CAR AN' WEAR BARBIE® CLOTHES!

AN' I WANT A BARBIE® BEDROOM, AN' A BARBIE® KITCHEN, AN' A BARBIE® BATHROOM!

THAT'S ALL..?? DON'T YOU WANT MORE OUT OF LIFE, ZOE?

OH YEAH... AN' A BARBIE® BOAT!

ATTAGIRL... SHOOT FOR THE STARS!

KIRKMAN & SCOTT

HMMM...DIRTY DISHES NEED TO BE PUT IN THE DISHWASHER.

BUT THE DISHWASHER IS STILL FULL OF CLEAN DISHES THAT NEED TO BE PUT AWAY.

WANDA IS BUSY WITH THE KIDS, SO THERE'S ONLY ONE LOGICAL THING TO DO...

KIRKMAN & SCOTT

...PUTTER AROUND IN THE GARAGE.

WHAT ARE YOU DOING OUT HERE WHEN THE HOUSE IS SUCH A MESS??

SORTING SCREWS.

SORTING SCREWS?? THERE'S A SINK FULL OF DIRTY DISHES, A MEAL TO COOK, A HOUSE TO CLEAN, LAUNDRY TO DO, TWO KIDS THAT NEED TO BE ENTERTAINED, AND **YOU** DECIDE TO SORT SCREWS?? **WHY??**

BECAUSE THERE'S A SINK FULL OF DIRTY DISHES, A MEAL TO COOK, A HOUSE TO CLEAN, LAUNDRY TO DO...

THEY SAY THEY WANT YOU TO TELL THEM THE TRUTH, BUT THEY REALLY DON'T.

YEAH. OKAY. BYE.

WHO WAS THAT?

SOME CHARITY SOLICITING DONATIONS...

WHAT DID YOU SAY?

I TOLD THEM THAT WE HAVE ONE INCOME, TWO KIDS, A MORTGAGE, CAR PAYMENT, CREDIT CARD BILLS, AND FUTURE COLLEGE TUITION TO WORRY ABOUT, SO THINGS ARE REALLY TIGHT RIGHT NOW.

I HOPE THEY UNDERSTAND...

THEY'RE DROPPING OFF FIFTY BUCKS AND AN OLD SOFA.

♪ HI, HAMMIEEE! ARE YOU ALL DWESSED? HUH? ♪

♪ YOU LOOK SOOO NICE! ♪ YES YOU DO!

I'M GLAD YOU LIKE HAMMIE'S OUTFIT, ZOE... IT USED TO BE YOURS.

DID **I** WEAR **BOY** CLOTHES, OR IS **HE** WEARING **GIRL** CLOTHES?

BABY BLUES®

BY RICK KIRKMAN / JERRY SCOTT

LOOK! WE GOT ZOE'S PRESCHOOL CLASS PICTURES!

ISN'T THIS CUTE? THE KIDS TRADED PICTURES WITH EACH OTHER ALREADY!

WHY IS THAT KID CHEWING ON A SNEAKER?

THAT'S BRYAN THE DINOSAUR, AND HE'S ALWAYS HUNGRY.

AN' THAT'S KENNY THE PASTE-EATER...

"...GWEN THE SCREAMER, JAKE THE WHINER, JENNIFER THE GRABBER..."

DOES EVERY KID THERE HAVE A NICKNAME?

MEET ZOE THE FILM-WASTER.

WANT ONE?

128